our wonderful
weather

valerie bodden

hurricanes

creative ☾ education

our wonderful
weather

Published by Creative Education
P.O. Box 227, Mankato, Minnesota 56002
Creative Education is an imprint of The Creative Company
www.thecreativecompany.us

Design and production by Christine Vanderbeek
Art direction by Rita Marshall
Printed by Corporate Graphics in the United States of America

Photographs by 123RF (Odessa4), Alamy (Neil Cooper, Corbis RF, Mike Hill, J Marshall-Tribaleye
Images, Photoshot Holdings Ltd), Corbis (Alejandro Ernesto, Jim Reed Photography, John Lund,
Eric Nguyen, Reuters), Dreamstime (Greg Blomberg, Christy Thompson), Getty Images (Don Emmert/
AFP, David A. Harvey/National Geographic, Jacqueline Hunkele, Johner, Nicholas Kamm/AFP, Paul
J. Richards/AFP, Orlando Sierra/AFP, Erik Simonsen), iStockphoto (Lisa Barreca, Mike Bentley,
Donald Johansson, Seraficus, vm, Hande Guleryuz Yuce)

Library of Congress Cataloging-in-Publication Data

Bodden, Valerie.
Hurricanes / by Valerie Bodden.
Summary: A simple exploration of hurricanes, examining how these massive sea storms develop,
how scientists watch for them and measure their strength, and the damage hurricanes can cause.
Includes bibliographical references and index.
ISBN 978-1-60818-147-6
1. Hurricanes—Juvenile literature. I. Title.
QC944.2.B63 2012
551.55'2—dc22   2010052762

CPSIA: 030513 PO1659

468975

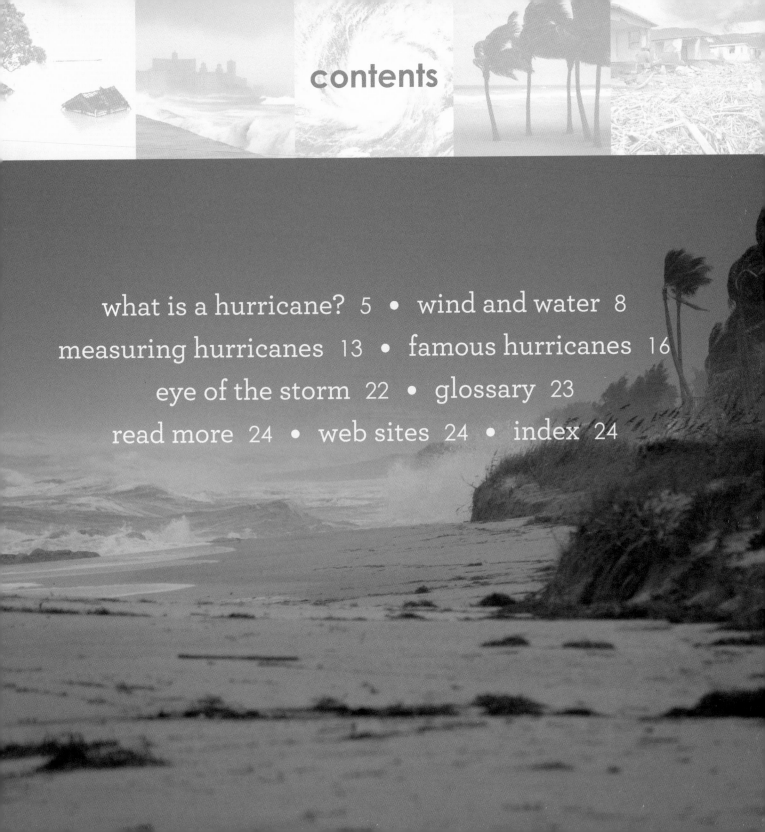

contents

A hurricane is a huge, circle-shaped storm over the ocean. Hurricanes form when warm water evaporates from the ocean and becomes water vapor. The water vapor rises into the sky and forms clouds.

Water from the ocean helps to form big storm clouds

Sometimes, these clouds form a storm that begins to spin. If the storm's winds blow fast enough, it becomes a hurricane. Hurricanes can blow across the ocean for many days. Sometimes they reach land.

Hurricanes can bring very strong winds and waves to land

The middle of a hurricane is called the eye. The eye is calm and sunny. But outside the eye, hurricane winds blow.

eye of a hurricane

Heavy rains fall. If the hurricane reaches land, a wall of seawater called the storm surge rises up and covers the ground.

storm surge

Some hurricanes are 50 miles (80 km) from one side to the other. Other hurricanes are much bigger. They can be 600 miles (966 km) across!

A hurricane can hurt trees and land across a very big area

Meteorologists (mee-tee-uh-RAH-luh-jists) are people who study weather. They try to forecast how the weather will change. They use satellites to see where hurricanes are forming. Then airplanes may fly to the area and drop tools into the storm to measure its strength.

Satellites can take pictures of storm clouds and the ocean

Hurricanes are measured by their winds and storm surge. Category 1 hurricanes have winds of 74 to 95 miles (119–153 km) per hour and a low storm surge.

The strongest hurricanes are Category 5. They have winds faster than 155 miles (249 km) per hour and a high storm surge.

In 1992, Hurricane Andrew hit Florida and Louisiana. It was a Category 5 storm that killed 23 people. In 2005, Hurricane

Hurricane Andrew

Katrina hit Louisiana and the area around it. It was only a Category 2 storm, but it killed more than 1,500 people.

Hurricane Katrina

Most of the people killed in hurricanes die in floods. Floods are caused by storm surges and rain. Hurricane winds can knock down trees, power lines, and buildings.

New Orleans, Louisiana, was flooded by Hurricane Katrina

If you live near the ocean, you need to be ready for hurricanes. If a strong hurricane is forecast, you might have to evacuate (ee-VA-kyoo-wayt). It can be very dangerous to be in the way of these powerful storms!

EYE OF THE STORM

You can make your own spinning hurricane. First, fill a large, round bowl with water. Move a spoon in a circle near the edge of the bowl to stir the water. Once the water is spinning quickly, stop stirring. Add about three drops of food coloring to the middle of the bowl. Watch as the food coloring "clouds" spin around the eye of your mini-hurricane!

GLOSSARY

evacuate — to leave a dangerous place and go somewhere safer

evaporates — changes from a liquid (such as water) into a vapor, or liquid drops so tiny that they rise into the air

floods — large amounts of water that cover land that is usually dry

forecast — to try to figure out what is going to happen in the future, such as during the next day or week

power lines — wires that hang from tall poles and carry electricity to homes and other buildings

satellites — machines that circle Earth in space; weather satellites can take pictures of clouds and measure temperatures

water vapor — water that has turned into drops so tiny that it rises into the air and becomes invisible

READ MORE

Harris, Caroline. *Science Kids: Weather*. London: Kingfisher, 2009.

Manolis, Kay. *Hurricanes*. Minneapolis: Bellwether Media, 2009.

WEB SITES

Associated Press Interactive: Hurricanes History

http://hosted.ap.org/specials/interactives/_national/
hurricanesHistoryNew/ index.html
Learn about the damage different categories of hurricanes
can cause.

FEMA for Kids: Hurricanes

http://www.fema.gov/kids/hurr.htm
Learn more about how to stay safe during a hurricane.

INDEX